For Alison Cinder, Jim
and Marshall Rice
with warm wishes

Feb '98

Manhattan Seascape

Waterside Views Around New York

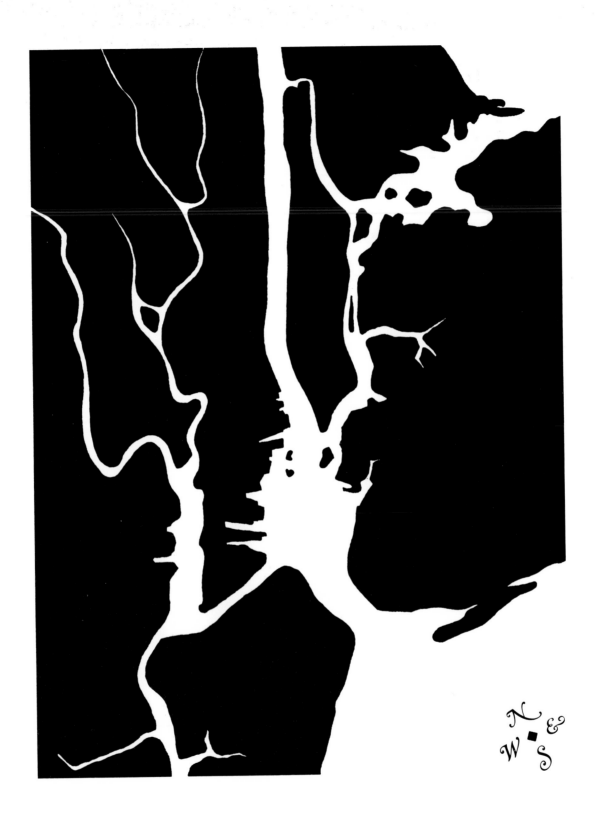

Manhattan Seascape

Waterside Views Around New York

Robert Gambee

Hastings House, Publishers • New York

For Susan

Published simultaneously in Canada
by Saunders of Toronto Ltd.
Don Mills, Ontario

Library of Congress Cataloging in Publication Data
Main entry under title:

Manhattan seascape.

1. American literature.   2. New York (City)—
Literary collections.   3.   Waterfronts—New York (City)
—Literary collections.   I.   Gambee, Robert.
PS509.N5M3   811′.5′408032   75-16267
ISBN 0-8038-5043-3

Printed by Rapoport Printing Corp., New York, N.Y.

Photographic Consultation: Diana Mara Henry

Design: Dave Epstein

Preface

What every New Yorker really needs is a book about New England cross country skiing or maybe white water canoeing down the Snake River—certainly not another book about the one place many of us strive to forget. That's the way I felt about New York for a long time. In fact for many years my favorite weekend pastime in the city was to leave. Along with everyone else.

But after a while I started to become more aware of my native city and especially so during the energy crisis of 1973–1974 when weekend escapes became so restricted. I began to look around and to photograph, and as I photographed I looked, and then I began to see. What was it about New York and its harbor that made this the greatest city in the world? This was the question I kept asking myself again and again. My answer is expressed in the photographs—many of which continue to amaze me, not because of the pictures themselves but because of the subject matter. Every sight I thought I knew so well by heart changed completely when approached from a different angle. (How many thousands of times have you crossed the Henry Hudson Bridge? How many times have you been under it—by the Spuyten Duyvil train stop? It's the same bridge but down there it's another world.)

It was confirmed during my quest that New York was a city of power and vitality. "New York, New York—a city so great they went and named it twice," an Atlanta bootblack wisely told me one time. But in the process of photographing I discovered new views of New York I never knew existed. Especially the magnificent harbor. Something once so important to everyone coming and going from this city and now virtually taken for granted and ignored. All of Manhattan is ringed with water and docks and parks and vistas that are spellbinding, yet to the average one of us we might as well be in Nebraska for all the water we actually come into contact with.

The majority of the photographs were taken during the years 1972 to 1975. Harbor shots were made from various shorelines with regular and long lenses or from the ferries and public excursion boats. While I did make a few trips with the McAllister and Moran tugboat people, I never felt the need to charter a boat to move about the waterfronts. All of the places photographed are accessible to anyone by bus and subway, or bicycle, or in a few cases due to convenience—by car (especially the outlying areas).

Collected thus are views of the city which are available to every New Yorker who is interested in viewing. New York: the grand, the magnificent—with its architecture, vitality and sweep of its harbor. Also New York: the personal, the friendly, the peaceful . . . another town, another place that has been with us all along. And this was perhaps the most exciting discovery of my venture. But it should have been no real surprise, because after all a peaceful setting creates a state of mind that in turn opens up a greater awareness of things than was at first apparent. A new set of views of the city seemed to spring out of the old ones. And therefore, working together: the camera, the eyes, the mind and the mood—these elements brought new sights and a general serenity that was as great walking down a path by the Hudson, for example, as one might expect from a stroll in Vermont.

These photographs are personal recordings of what I felt, just as the accompanying poems and prose reflect the views of their respective authors. However, feelings are so subjective that one should strive to see according to one's own eyes. People often talk about photographs conveying feelings and ideas. But there is no necessary correlation between what the photographer intends to communicate and what the viewer sees. That is why I hope the readers of this book will be inspired to see for themselves what it is about New York that is interesting or moving to them. In so doing I hope more and more people will grow to appreciate this unique city, and in the process of ignoring it less, or even downgrading it less, they will find greater contentment within themselves.

R.G.

Table of Contents

Manhattan Seascape

Waterside Views Around New York

Mannahatta

I was asking for something specific and perfect for my
    city,
Whereupon lo! upsprang the aboriginal name.

Now I see what there is in a name, a word, liquid,
    sane, unruly, musical, self-sufficient,
I see that the word of my city is that word from of
    old,
Because I see that word nested in nests of water-bays,
    superb,
Rich, hemm'd thick all around with sailships and
    steamships, an island sixteen miles long, solid-founded,
Numberless crowded streets, high growths of iron, slender,
    strong, light, splendidly uprising toward clear skies,
Tides swift and ample, well-loved by me, toward
    sundown,
The flowing sea-currents, the little islands, larger
    adjoining islands, the heights, the villas,
The countless masts, the white shore-steamers, the lighters,
    the ferry-boats, the black sea-steamers well-model'd,
The down-town streets, the jobbers' houses of business,
    the houses of business of the ship-merchants
    and money-brokers, the river-streets,
Immigrants arriving, fifteen or twenty thousand in a
    week,
The carts hauling goods, the manly race of drivers of
    horses, the brown-faced sailors,
The summer air, the bright sun shining, and the sailing
    clouds aloft,
The winter snows, the sleigh-bells, the broken ice in the river,
    passing along up or down with the flood-tide or ebb-tide,
The mechanics of the city, the masters, well-form'd,
    beautiful-faced, looking you straight in the eyes,
Trottoirs throng'd, vehicles, Broadway, the women,
    the shops and shows,
A million people—manners free and supurb—open voices—
    hospitality—the most courageous and friendly young men,
City of hurried and sparkling waters! city of spires
    and masts!
City nested in bays! my city!

Walt Whitman

Around the Great Port

There stands Manhattan like an island keep, a fortress of power, talent, greed and beauty. Elderly ships' captains tell me they never lose the excitement of this moment, as they turn the corner of the Narrows beneath the bridge, and see this sight before them. Tired commuters taking the ferry home to Staten Island still stand silent on the windy stern to watch the lights of Manhattan retreat into the night. Blasé diplomatists flying in from Europe press their noses to the window, when the towers of New York are sighted through the haze. We read of voyagers dropping dead of heart attacks, like pilgrims reaching Mecca, or explorers crossing the threshholds of Lhasa. . . .

The adjectives that normally go with seaports—robust, breezy, hearty—scarcely apply to New York. This is not only temperament, but topography too, for the New Yorkers have largely wrecked their own waterfronts and shut the sea breezes out. There was seldom a more wonderfully situated metropolis, set upon its double bay within sight of the ocean, with the ships docking just down the road from the concert halls and couturiers. It is still a thrilling fact that the largest of the world's liners tie up within a mile of the Metropolitan Opera House—"as though one of our ships were to sail," a Cunard man once suggested to me, "bang up Piccadilly to dock in Trafalgar Square." There are lesser capitals—Stockholm, Reykjavik—where the ships come even closer to the center of things, and the parliamentarian emerging from his debate may see the prow of a freighter almost immediately outside the legislative door, to prod him into support for shipping subsidies; but I know of no other supreme metropolis where the ships lie so intimately close to the heart of urban life. . . . I suppose there is no human artifact that greets you more absolutely than Manhattan, as your ship swings through the Narrows into the Bay, or your helicopter scuds past Tompkinsville. Grand and uncompromising the skyscrapers stand there, in a miasma of movement around their feet, windows flashing in the sunshine, aerials prodding the sky, radars twirling, jets streaking this way and that. At first I had seen this incomparable spectacle as an exclamation mark, a shout of triumph from the New World. Later it seemed to me an interrogative—where are we bound for? Is our course right?

And so in the end I was left, like so many voyagers before me, trapped by the great port. I loathed it like a lover. The questions it asked I resented; the answers it gave I mistrusted; the spell of it, the chivvying of conscience, the temptations, the delight, I felt to be unfair. Damn you, New York! Damn the bright sweep of your spaces, and the ungainly poetry of your names! A curse on all your archipelago, and on those rough fresh winds off your Bay—which catching me like an embrace as I stepped out of the helicopter, so often ravished my spirits, and made my heart sing!

J. H. Morris
The Great Port

The Bay

It is indubitably a "great" bay, a great harbor, but no one item of the romantic, or even of the picturesque, as commonly understood, contributes to its effect. The shores are low and for the most part prosaically peopled; the islands, though numerous, have not a grace to exhibit, and one thinks of the other, the real flowers of geography in this order, of Naples, of Capetown, of Sydney, of Seattle, of San Francisco, of Rio, asking how if *they* justify a reputation, New York should seem to justify one. Then, after all, we remember that there are reputations and reputations; we remember above all that the imaginative response to the conditions here presented may just happen to proceed from the intellectual extravagance of the given observer. . . . There is the beauty of light and air, the great scale of space, and, seen far away to the west, the open gates of the Hudson, majestic in their degree, even at a distance, and announcing still nobler things. But the real appeal, unmistakably, is in that note of vehemence in

the local life of which I have spoken, for it is the appeal of a particular type of dauntless power.

The aspect the power wears then is indescribable; it is the power of the most extravagant of cities, rejoicing, as with the voice of the morning, in its might, its fortune, its unsurpassable conditions, and imparting to every object and element, to the motion and expression of every floating, hurrying, panting thing, to the throb of ferries and tugs, to the plash of waves and the play of winds and the glint of lights and the shrill of whistles and the quality and authority of breeze-borne cries—all, practically, a diffused, wasted clamor of detonations—something of its sharp free accent and, above all, of its sovereign sense of being "backed" and able to back. The universal applied passion struck me as shining unprecedentedly out of the composition; in the bigness and bravery and insolence, especially, of everything that rushed and shrieked; in the air as of a great intricate frenzied dance, half merry, half desperate, or at least half defiant, performed on the huge watery floor. This appearance of the bold lacing-together, across the waters, of the scattered members of the monstrous organism—lacing as by the ceaseless play of an enormous system of steam-shuttles or electric bobbins (I scarce know what to call them), commensurate in form with their infinite work—does perhaps more than anything else to give the pitch of the vision of energy. . . . The immeasurable bridges are but as the horizontal sheaths of pistons working at high pressure, day and night, and subject, one apprehends with perhaps inconsistent gloom, to certain, to fantastic, to merciless multiplication. In the light of this apprehension indeed the breezy brightness of the Bay puts on the semblance of the vast white page that awaits beyond any other perhaps the black overscoring of science.

Let me hasten to add that its present whiteness is precisely its charming note, the frankest of the signs you recognize and remember it by. That is the distinction I was just feeling my way to name as the main ground of its doing so well, for effect, without technical scenery. There are great imposing ports—Glasgow and Liverpool and London—that have already their page blackened almost beyond redemption from any such light of the picturesque as can hope to irradiate fog and grime, and there are others, Marseilles and Constantinople say, or, for all I know to the contrary, New Orleans, that contrive to abound before everything else in color, and so to make a rich and instant and obvious show. *But memory and the actual impression keep investing New York with the tone, predominantly, of summer dawns and winter frosts, of sea-foam, of bleached sails and stretched awnings, of blanched hulls, of scoured decks, of new ropes, of polished brasses, of streamers clear in the blue air; and it is by this harmony, doubtless, that the projection of the individual character of the place, of the candor of its avidity and the freshness of its audacity, is most conveyed.*

Henry James
The American Scene

The Harbor Dawn

Insistently through sleep—a tide of voices—
They meet you listening midway in your dream,
The long, tired sounds, fog-insulated noises:
Gongs in white surplices, beshrouded wails,
Far strum of fog horns . . . signals dispersed in veils.

And then a truck will lumber past the wharves
As winch engines begin throbbing on some deck;
Or a drunken stevedore's howl and thud below
Comes echoing alley-upward through dim snow.

And if they take your sleep away sometimes
They give it back again. Soft sleeves of sound
Attend the darkling harbor, the pillowed bay;
Somewhere out there in blankness steam

Spills into steam, and wanders, washed away
—Flurried by keen fifings, eddied
Among distant chiming buoys—adrift. The sky,
Cool feathery fold, suspends, distills
This wavering slumber . . . Slowly—
Immemorially the window, the half-covered chair
Ask nothing but this sheath of pallid air.

And you beside me, blessed now while sirens
Sing to us, stealthily weave us into day—
Serenely now, before day claims our eyes
Your cool arms murmurously about me lay.

While myriad snowy hands are clustering at the
        panes—
        your hands within my hands are deeds;
        my tongue upon your throat—singing
        arms close; eyes wide, undoubtful
                dark
                        drink the dawn—
        a forest shudders in your hair!

The window goes blond slowly. Frostily clears.
From Cyclopean towers across Manhattan waters
—Two—three bright window-eyes aglitter, disk
The sun, released—aloft with cold gulls hither.

The fog leans one last moment on the sill.
Under the mistletoe of dreams, a star—
As though to join us at some distant hill—
Turns in the waking west and goes to sleep.

*400 years and
more . . . or is
it from the
soundless shore
of sleep that
time*

*recalls you to
your love,
there in a waking
dream to
merge your seed*

—with whom?

*Who is the
woman with
us in the
dawn? . . .
whose is the
flesh our feet
have moved
upon?*

Hart Crane

East River Morning: View from the Author's Window

Everything was touched with morning, and the river was flashing with all the ecstasy and movement of its thousand currents. . . . The tide was coming in upon the full. . . . It was a steady, flowing, crawling and impulsive surge—a welling flood that would come on forever and knew no limit to the invasion of its power. The river was not quiet; the tide was ruffled by the breath of morning into a million scallop-shells of winking light—rose, golden, silver, sapphire, pink—the whole polychrome of morning was reflected in the stream, and within the channel of the river's life, the tide came on. . . . A tug, set neatly in between two barges, each loaded with twin rows of box-cars, backed out into the stream and quartered slowly, steadily, with its enormous freight, then started head-on up the stream. Thick water foamed against the blunt snouts of the barges, as the little tug between them neatly forged ahead with its great cargo, with a sense of limitless power, and with astonishing speed. The young cool light of morning fell flat and cleanly on the rusty sides of the old freight cars on the barges: everything began to blaze with thrilling color. The excitement, the beauty, the feelings of wonder and recognition which all of the associations of the scene evoked, were intoxicating.

Thomas Wolfe
No More Rivers

On the Ferryboat

The ferryboat into the waters dim
    Slipped forward with a sound of churning foam;
    Studded with stars, hung low the heaven's dome
Around them—and along the city's rim,

Over the shadowed river's murky flowing,
    Glittered a million lights of starry sheen;
    Sharp whiffs and ocean odors, salt and keen,
Swept up the east, and sullen whistles blowing

In from the sea-gate, from the ocean ways.
    Past dock and dock, past lamp and flaring lamp,
    They glided into the twilight chill and damp,
Over the waters, through the ghostly haze,

Over the lifting and the lapsing tide,
    And left the city lying sleeplessly
    At the soft bosom of the heaving sea,
At the bosom of the everlasting bride.

The silence and the engirdling solitude
    Drew them together closer, more and more;
    Never had he observed her thus before,
So grave and yet so merry was her mood,

So tender, yet so merry: all her speech
    Was glad by turns and sad, like April weather—
    Close, on the upper deck, they sat together,
Each lost within the happiness of each.

No less than if an enchanted boat
    They had sought beyond the stars a fairy realm
    Of mosques and minarets, Love at the helm
And joys for oarsmen, on the waves afloat,

They were embarked and drifted on the stream
    Of night and waves, beyond the hand of day
    And all its cares—cut loose and cut away,
With steering prow, into the dusk of dream.

And now at some new wonder, as they went,
    Unveiled before them, with delight they sprang
    To scan the waters; now their laughter rang;
Now they sat wordless in a deep content.

Around them reached the gray and glimmering shore—
    Fortress headland, tower and lamp warning,
    The sea-road to the worlds beyond the morning,
Behind them, and the eternal stars before.

John Hall Wheelock

From the Ferryboat

They came out on deck into a dazzling September afternoon. The water was greenindigo. A steady wind kept sweeping coils of brown smoke and blobs of whitecotton steam off the high enormous blueindigo arch of sky. Against a sootsmudged horizon, tangled with barges, steamers, chimneys of powerplants, covered wharves, bridges, lower New York was a pink and white tapering pyramid cut slenderly out of cardboard. . . .

Across the zinc water the tall walls, the birchlike cluster of downtown buildings shimmered up the rosy morning like a sound of horns through a chocolatebrown haze. As the boat drew near the buildings densened to a granite mountain split with knifecut canyons. The ferry passed close to a tubby steamer that rode at anchor listing towards Stan so that he could see all the decks. An Ellis Island tug was alongside. A stale smell came from the decks packed with upturned faces like a load of melons. The gulls wheeled complaining. A gull soared in a spiral, white wings caught the sun, the gull skimmed motionless in whitegold light. The rim of the sun had risen above the plumcolored band of clouds behind East New York. A million windows flashed with light. A rasp and a humming came from the city. . . .

In the whitening light tinfoil gulls wheeled above broken boxes, spoiled cabbageheads, orangerinds heaving slowly between the splintered plank walls, the green spumed under the round bow as the ferry skidding on the tide, gulped the broken water, crashed, slid, settled slowly into the slip. Handwinches whirled with jingle of chains, gates folded upward. . . .

There was Babylon and Nineveh, they were built of brick. Athens was goldmarble columns. Rome was held up on broad arches of rubble. In Constantinople the minarets flame like great candles round the Golden Horn. . . . Steel, glass, tile, concrete will be the materials of the skyscrapers. Crammed on the narrow island the millionwindowed buildings will jut, glittering pyramid on pyramid, white cloudsheads piled above a thunderstorm.

John Dos Passos
Manhattan Transfer

Crossing Brooklyn Ferry

1

Flood-tide below me! I watch you face to face;
Clouds of the west! sun there half an hour high! I see you also
      face to face.

Crowds of men and women attired in the usual costumes! how
      curious you are to me!
On the ferry-boats, the hundreds and hundreds that cross, re-
      turning home, are more curious to me than you suppose;
And you that shall cross from shore to shore years hence, are
      more to me, and more in my meditations, than you might suppose.

2

The impalpable sustenance of me from all things, at all hours of
      the day;
The simple, compact, well-join'd scheme—myself disintegrated,
      every one disintegrated, yet part of the scheme:
The similitudes of the past, and those of the future;
The glories strung like beads on my smallest sights and hearings
      —on the walk in the street, and the passage over the river;
The current rushing so swiftly, and swimming with me far
      away;
The others that are to follow me, the ties between me and them;
The certainty of others—the life, love, sight, hearing of others.

Others will enter the gates of the ferry, and cross from shore to
      shore;
Others will watch the run of the flood-tide;
Others will see the shipping of Manhattan north and west, and
      the heights of Brooklyn to the south and east;
Others will see the islands large and small;
Fifty years hence, others will see them as they cross, the sun
      half an hour high;
A hundred years hence, or ever so many hundred years hence,
      others will see them,
Will enjoy the sunset, the pouring in of the flood-tide, the fall-
      ing back to the sea of the ebb-tide.

3

It avails not, neither time or place—distance avails not;
I am with you, you men and women of a generation, or ever so
      many generations hence;
I project myself—also I return—I am with you, and know how it is.

Just as you feel when you look on the river and sky, so I felt;
Just as any of you is one of a living crowd, I was one of a crowd;
Just as you are refresh'd by the gladness of the river and the
        bright flow, I was refresh'd;
Just as you stand and lean on the rail, yet hurry with the swift
        current, I stood, yet was hurried;
Just as you look on the numberless masts of ships, and the thick-
        stem'd pipes of steamboats, I look'd.

I too many and many a time cross'd the river, the sun half an hour high;
I watched the Twelfth-month sea-gulls—I saw them high in the
        air, floating with motionless wings, oscillating their bodies,
I saw how the glistening yellow lit up parts of their bodies, and
        left the rest in strong shadow,
I saw the slow-wheeling circles, and the gradual edging toward the south.

I too saw the reflection of the summer sky in the water,
Had my eyes dazzled by the shimmering track of beams,
Look'd at the fine centrifugal spokes of light around the shape
        of my head in the sun-lit water,
Look'd on the haze on the hills southward and southwestward,
Look'd on the vapor as it flew in fleeces tinged with violet,
Look'd toward the lower bay to notice the arriving ships,
Saw their approach, saw aboard those that were near me,
Saw the white sails of schooners and sloops—saw the ships at
        anchor,
The sailors at work in the rigging, or out astride the spars,
The round masts, the swinging motion of the hulls, the slender
        serpentine pennants,
The large and small steamers in motion, the pilots in their pilot-
        houses,
The white wake left by the passage, the quick tremulous whirl
        of the wheels,
The flags of all nations, the falling of them at sun-set,
The scallop-edged waves in the twilight, the ladled cups, the
        frolicsome crests and glistening,
The stretch afar growing dimmer and dimmer, the gray walls of
        the granite store-houses by the docks. . . .

4

These, and all else, were to me the same as they are to you;
I project myself a moment to tell you—also I return.

Walt Whitman
(abridged)

The New Colossus

Not like the brazen giant of Greek fame,
With conquering limbs astride from land to land;
Here at our sea-washed, sunset gates shall stand
A mighty woman with a torch whose flame
Is the imprisoned lightning, and her name
Mother of Exiles. From her beacon-hand
Glows world-wide welcome; her mild eyes command
The air-bridged harbor that twin cities frame.
"Keep, ancient lands, your storied pomp!" cries she
With silent lips. "Give me your tired, your poor,
Your huddled masses yearning to breathe free,
The wretched refuse of your teeming shore.
Send these, the homeless, tempest-tossed to me,
I lift my lamp beside the golden door!"

Emma Lazarus

2. Downtown

Wall Street, South Street

This narrow thoroughfare, baking and blistering in
the sun, is Wall Street: the Stock Exchange and Lombard
Street of New York. Many a rapid fortune has been made
in this street, and many a no less rapid ruin. Some
of these very merchants whom you see hanging about here
now, have locked up money in their strong-boxes, like
the man in the Arabian Nights, and opening them again,
have found but withered leaves. Below, here by the waterside,
where the bowsprits of ships stretch across the footway,
and almost thrust themselves into the windows, lie the
noble American vessels which have made their Packet
Service the finest in the world. They have brought hither
the foreigners who abound in all the streets: not, perhaps,
that there are more here than in other commercial cities;
but elsewhere they have particular haunts, and you must
find them out; here they pervade the town.

Charles Dickens
American Notes

City of Ships

City of ships!
(O the black ships! O the fierce ships!
O the beautiful sharp-bow'd steamships and
    sailships!)
City of the world! (for all races are here,
All the lands of the earth make contributions
    here;)
City of the sea! city of hurried and glittering
    tides!
City whose gleeful tides
    continually rush or recede,
    whirling in and out with eddies and foam!
City of wharves and stores—city of tall facades of
    marble and iron!
Proud and passionate city—meddlesome, mad,
    extravagant city!
Spring up, O city—not for peace alone, but be indeed
    yourself, warlike!
Fear not—submit to no models but your own, O
    city!
Behold me—incarnate me as I have incarnated
    you!
I have rejected nothing you offer'd me—whom you
    adopted I have adopted,
Good or bad I never question you—I love all—I do
    not condemn anything,
I chant and celebrate all that is yours—yet peace no
    more,
In peace I chanted peace, but now the drum of war is
    mine,
War, red war is my song through your streets, O
    city!

Walt Whitman

Manhattan from the Bay

June 25.—Returned to New York last night. Out to-day on the waters for a sail in the wide bay, southeast of Staten island—a rough, tossing ride, and a free sight—the long stretch of Sandy Hook, the highlands of Navesink, and the many vessels outward and inward bound. We came up through the midst of all, in the full sun. I especially enjoy'd the last hour or two. A moderate sea-breeze had set in; yet over the city, and the waters adjacent, was a thin haze, concealing nothing, only adding to the beauty. From my point of view, as I write amid the soft breeze, with a sea-temperature, surely nothing on earth of its kind can go beyond this show. To the left the North River with its far vista—nearer, three or four war-ships, anchor'd peacefully—the Jersey side, the banks of Weehawken, the Palisades, and the gradually receding blue, lost in the distance—to the right the East river—the mast-hemmed shores—the grand obelisk-like towers of the bridge, one on either side, in haze, yet plainly defin'd, giant brothers twain, throwing free graceful interlinking loops high across the tumbled tumultuous current below—(the tide is just changing to its ebb)—the broad water-spread everywhere crowded—no, not crowded, but thick as stars in the sky—with all sorts and sizes of sail and steam vessels, plying ferryboats, arriving and departing coasters, great ocean Dons, iron-black, modern, magnificent in size and power, fill'd with their incalculable value of human life and precious merchandise—with here and there, above all, those daring, careening things of grace and wonder, those white and shaded swift-darting fish-birds, (I wonder if shore or sea elsewhere can outvie them,) ever with their slanting spars, and fierce, pure, hawk-like beauty and motion—first-class New York sloop or schooner yachts, sailing, this fine day, the free sea in a good wind. And rising out of the midst, tall-topt, ship-hemmed, modern, American, yet strangely oriental, V-shaped Manhattan, with its compact mass, its spires, its cloud-touching edifices group'd at the centre—the green of the trees, and all the white, brown and gray of the architecture well blended, as I see it, under a miracle of limpid sky, delicious light of heaven above, and June haze on the surface below.

Walt Whitman
Specimen Days

The Water Gazers

There now is your insular city of the Manhattoes, belted round by wharves as Indian isles by coral reefs—commerce surrounds it with her surf. Right and left, the streets take you waterward. Its extreme down-town is the Battery, where that noble mole is washed by waves, and cooled by breezes, which a few hours previous were out of sight of land.

Circumambulate the city on a dreamy Sabbath afternoon. Go from Corlears Hook to Coenties Slip, and from thence, by Whitehall, northward. What do you see?—Posted like silent sentinels all around the town, stand thousands upon thousands of mortal men fixed in ocean reveries. Some leaning against the piles; some seated upon the pier-heads; some looking over the bulwarks of ships from China; some high aloft in the rigging, as if striving to get a still better seaward peep. But these are all landsmen; of week days pent up in lath and plaster—tied to counters, nailed to benches, clinched to desks. How then is this? Are the green fields gone? What do they here?

But look! here come more crowds, pacing straight for the water, and seemingly bound for a dive. Strange! Nothing will content them but the extremest limit of the land; loitering under the shady lee of yonder warehouses will not suffice. No. They must get just as nigh the water as they possibly can without falling in. And there they stand—miles of them—leagues. Inlanders all, they come from lanes and alleys, streets and avenues—north, east, south, and west. Yet here they all unite. Tell me, does the magnetic virtue of the needles of the compasses of all those ships attract them thither?

Herman Melville
Moby Dick

On the Quay

I've never traveled for more'n a day,
    I never was one to roam,
        But I likes to sit on the busy quay,
        Watchin' the ships that says to me—
"Always somebody goin' away,
    Somebody gettin' home."

I likes to think that the world's so wide—
    'Tis grand to be livin' there,
        Takin' a part in its goin's on. . . .
        Ah, now you're laughin' at poor old John,
Talkin' o' works o' the world wi' pride
    As if he was doin' his share!

But laugh if ye will! When ye're old as me
    Ye'll find 'tis a rare good plan
        To look at the world—an' love it too!
        Though never a job are ye fit to do. . . .
Oh! 'tisn't all sorrow an' pain to see
    The work o' another man.

'Tis good when the heart grows big at last,
    Too big for trouble to fill—
        Wi' room for the things that was only stuff
        When workin' an' winnin' seemed more'n enough—
Room for the world, the world so vast
    Wi' its peoples an' all their skill.

That's what I'm thinkin' on all the days
    I'm loafin' an' smokin' here,
        An' the ships do make me think the most
        (Of readin' in books 'tis little I'd boast)—
But the ships, they carries me long, long ways,
    An' draws far places near.

I see the things that a sailor brings,
    I hears the stories he tells. . . .
        'Tis surely a wonderful world indeed!
        'Tis more'n the peoples can ever need!
An I praises the Lord—to myself I sings—
    For the world in which I dwells.

An' I loves the ships more every day,
    Though I never was one to roam.
        Oh! the ships is comfortin' sights to see,
        An' they means a lot when they says to me—
"Always somebody goin' away,
    Somebody gettin' home."

John Joy Bell

Old St. Paul's

Park Row and Broadway—rush and din,
    Turmoil of men in their strong, brief years,
Conquest, honor, failure and sin!—
    Rest for a moment the eyes and the ears;
Step through this gate for a while with me
Where struggles pause, and thought is free.

Look at the words on this little stone
    Under the trees of old St. Paul's.
Ninety summers have flowered and flown,
    Round these ivied Georgian walls,
Since they cut in the headstone grey
The name of "Antipass Hathaway."

Only fourteen! Boy-gladness, his,
    Touched—would you say?—by the lips of joy
Into eternal youthfulness—
    Spirit abiding forever boy!
"March 29th,"—so they brought him here
In the very bud of the welling year.

Across the walk, quaint-carven French,
    Line after line in martial row,
Hinting at bivouac, storm, and trench
    Under the Comte de Rochambeau:
Valiant indeed, from far Champagne
Adventured the "Sieur de Rochefontaine."

Follow me over this stretch of sod;
    Mark the shaft with its moral urn;
There, where the red rose-bushes bud,
    A few spent petals, you notice, burn
Against the letters chiselled plain:
"Of the Theatre Royal, Drury Lane."

And a name now vague to you and me,
    An actor renowned in his day, forsooth;
See how they loved his memory:
    "Repaired by" . . . "Sothern," "Kean," and "Booth,"
"And by The Players"—Such fame's enough!
"Dreams" made his life: We are all "such stuff!"

Oh, but the schoolboy rolling hoops
    Over the grasses of Bowling Green,
And the brave young captain with his troops
    Charging into the battle-scene,
And the actor accomplished, praised by all—
Who gathered them here 'neath the churchyard wall?

Arthur Upson

3. The City of the Future

Earth, Water, Sky, Men

Any fair picture of New York must confess the underlying sordidness of a large part of its preoccupations and activities. It is not that manufacture and shipping and the exchange of goods are necessarily antivital or antisocial processes: quite the contrary. But when these activities become central to life, when they are themselves perverted to serve chiefly as instruments in an abstract accountancy of profit and power, the human hierarchy of values is displaced; and, as in some perversion of the physiological functions, the head becomes cretinous, and the subordinate members become gigantic *and useless*. What I have elsewhere called a purposeless materialism became the essential principle of the city's life.

One must not flinch, then, from recognizing the dark elements of the picture. But one would have no true image, in fact, no image at all, if one forgot to add the light and colors that define the blackest shape; and even at its worst, these elements were always present. There is, to begin with, the physical magnificence of the scene: the sweep and curve of the bay, the grand spaciousness of the river, the rhythm of the tides that encircle it, the strike of its mica-gleaming schists as they crop out in the park or the temporary excavation, and finally, the proud upthrust of the Palisades themselves. In the very shape of the island is something tight, lean, athletic: a contrast to the glacial till of Long Island, with its fat Dutch landscape, its duckponds, its feathery asparagus beds. The skyscrapers, despite their disorder, have not diminished those positive lines in their stalagmitic upthrust: they are almost as geometric as gypsum crystals. . . .

Above all, there is the sky; pervading all these activities is the weather. The sharp crystalline days of early autumn, with intense blue sky and a few curls of cloud, drifting through space like the little jets of steam that were once such characteristic outlets of the older skyscrapers: the splendors of sunset on the waters, over the Palisades, crossing the Brooklyn Ferry, looking toward the Jersey shore from the Brooklyn Bridge; the swift, whiplike changes from heat to cold, from fog to clarity, from the sharp jeweled contours of John Bellini to the soft tones of Whistler and Fuller. . . .

If the streets are dingy, there is the dazzle of the sky itself: if the alleys and yards are foul, heavy with ancient dirt, with the effluvia of the sewers or the factories, there is the sanative taste of salt in the first wind that blows from the Atlantic. The cold sea fog in spring, sweeping inland in the midafternoon, calls one to the ocean as imperatively as the proud, deep-throated roar of the steamer, claiming the channel as she passes out to sea. So the ocean and the sky and the rivers hold the city in their grip, even while the people, like busy ants in the cracks and crevices, are unconscious of these more primal presences, save when they read a report in the morning paper, and reach for an umbrella, an overcoat, a fan.

Lewis Mumford
City Development

New York, A Vertical but Incomplete City

New York is a vertical city, under the sign of the new times. It is a catastrophe with which a too hasty destiny has overwhelmed courageous and confident people, though a beautiful and worthy catastrophe. Nothing is lost. Faced with difficulties, New York falters. Still streaming with sweat from its exertions, wiping off its forehead, it sees what it has done and suddenly realizes: "Well, we didn't get it done properly. Let's start over again!" New York has such courage and enthusiasm that everything can be begun again, sent back to the building yard and made into something still greater, something mastered! These people are not on the point of going to sleep. In reality, the city is hardly more than twenty years old, that is the city which I am talking about, the city which is vertical and on the scale of the new times. . . .

It is the first time that men have projected all their strength and labor into the sky—a whole city in the free air of the sky. Good God, what disorder, what impetuosity! What perfection already, what promises! What unity in a molecular state, gridiron street plan, office on top of office, clear crystallization. It is sublime and atrocious, and nothing succeeds any longer. There is nothing to do except to see clearly, think, conceive, begin over again. Of course New York is ready to begin over again. Those people have courage!

That afternoon I had gone through the Holland Tunnel to the other side of the Hudson and over the Skyway, an elevated road so named because it rises on piles or arches high above industrial areas, arms of the sea, railways and roads, over an immense expanse. A road without art because no thought was given to it, but a wonderful tool. The "Skyway" rises up over the plain and leads to the "skyscrapers." Coming from the flat meadows of New Jersey, suddenly it reveals the City of the Incredible Towers. . . .

Suddenly New York has entered the family of the cities of the world, and not by the back door. The American is a Janus: one face absorbed by the anxieties of adolescence, looking toward the troubles of his consciousness; the other face as solid as an Olympic victor's, looking toward an old world which at certain moments he believes he can dominate. Reverse the situation: imagine in an urban drawing room a slightly awkward young man, sympathetic and hard-working, who has come a long way and who causes many well-established people to smile. One day his book, his speech, the battle he has won, explodes in the face of the world. He dominates. Look at his eyes: a hard flame of pride shines in them! Will he become an ass or a king?

New York is not a finished or completed city. It gushes up. On my next trip it will be different. Those of us who have visited it are asked this question: "When

you were there in 1939, or in 1928, or in 1926, or in 1920, was such and such already there? Oh, really, you don't know then what an effect that makes!" Such is the rhythm of the city. . . .

*   *   *

I shall come back to America. America is a great country. Hopeless cities and cities of hope at the same time. What an idea of the action between these two poles is thus expressed, what a battlefield is spread out between these two feelings which exist in the gasping heart of every man of action, of every man who believes enough in something to dare to attempt it, and who risks catastrophe for having wished to bring back trophies to the altar.

For, beyond the narrow limits of the average in human things, when magnitude enters into an undertaking (Assyrians, Hindus, Egyptians, Romans, and Gothic builders), the result becomes a public and civic thing and, like grace, makes a horror sublime.

All the French people whom I met on the ship going to New York, all those on this ship taking us back to Paris, resolve the question thus: "Once you have opened the door on America you cannot close it again."

Le Corbusier
When the Cathedrals Were White

The Pin Cushion of Tall Buildings

The "tall buildings," which have so promptly usurped a glory that affects you as rather surprised, as yet, at itself, the multitudinous sky-scrapers standing up to the view, from the water, like extravagant pins in a cushion already overplanted, and stuck in as in the dark, anywhere and anyhow, have at least the felicity of carrying out the fairness of tone, of taking the sun and the shade in the manner of towers of marble. They are not all of marble, I believe, by any means, even if some may be, but they are impudently new and still more impudently "novel"—this in common with so many other terrible things in America—and they are triumphant payers of dividends; all of which uncontested and unabashed pride, with flash of innumerable windows and flicker of subordinate gilt attributions, is like the flare, up and down their long, narrow faces, of the lamps of some general permanent "celebration."

You see the pin-cushion in profile, so to speak, on passing between Jersey City and Twenty-third Street, but you get it broadside on, this loose nosegay of architectural flowers, if you skirt the Battery, well out, and embrace the whole plantation. Then the "American beauty," the rose of interminable stem, becomes the token of the cluster at large—to that degree that, positively, this is all that is wanted for emphasis of your final impression. Such growths, you feel, have confessedly arisen but to be "picked," in time, with a shears; nipped short off, by waiting fate, as soon as "science," applied to gain, has put upon the table, from far up its sleeve, some winning card. Crowned not only with no history, but with no credible possibility of time for history, and consecrated by no uses save the commercial at any cost, they are simply the most piercing notes in that concert of the expensively provisional into which your supreme sense of New York resolves itself.

Henry James
The American Scene

The City of the Future

My first impressions of New York are enormously to enhance the effect of
this Progress, this material progress that is to say, as something inevitable and
inhuman, as a blindly furious energy of growth that must go on. Against the
broad and level grey contours of Liverpool one found the ocean liner porten-
tously tall, but here one steams into the middle of a town that dwarfs the ocean
liner. The skyscrapers that are the New Yorker's perpetual boast and pride rise
up to greet one as one comes through the Narrows into the Upper Bay, stand out
in a clustering group of tall irregular crenellations, the strangest crown that ever
a city wore. They have an effect of immense incompleteness; each one seems to
await some needed terminal,—to be, by virtue of its woolly jets of steam, still as it
were in process of eruption. One thinks of St. Peter's great blue dome, finished
and done as one saw it from a vine-shaded wine-booth above the Milvian Bridge,
one thinks of the sudden ascendency of St. Paul's dark grace, as it soars out over
any one who comes up by the Thames towards it. These are efforts that have
accomplished their ends, and even Paris illuminated under the tall stem of the
Eiffel Tower looked completed and defined. But New York's achievement is a
threatening promise, growth going on under a pressure that increases, and
amidst a hungry uproar of effort. . . .

Happy returning natives greet the great pillars of business by name, the St.
Paul Building, the World, the Manhattan tower; the English newcomer notes the
clear emphasis of the detail, the freedom from smoke and atmospheric mystery
that New York gains by burning anthracite, the jetting white steam clouds that
emphasise that freedom. Across the broad harbor plies an unfamiliar traffic of
grotesque broad ferry-boats, black with people, glutted to the lips with vans and
carts, each hooting and yelping its own distinctive note, and there is a wild
hurrying up and down and to and fro of piping and bellowing tugs and barges;
and a great floating platform, bearing a railway-train, gets athwart our course as
we ascend and evokes megatherial bellowings. Everything is moving at a great
speed and whistling and howling it seems, and presently far ahead we make out
our own pier, black with expectant people, and set up our own distinctive whoop,
and with the help of half-a-dozen furiously noisy tugs are finally 'lugged and
butted into dock. The tugs converse by yells and whistles, it is an affair of
short-tempered mechanical monsters, amidst which one watches for one's opportunity to get ashore.

Noise and human hurry and a vastness of means and collective result, rather
than any vastness of achievement, is the pervading quality of New York. The
great thing is the mechanical thing, the unintentional thing which is speeding up

all these people, driving them in headlong hurry this way and that, exhorting them by the voice of every car-conductor to "step lively," aggregating them into shoving and elbowing masses, making them stand clinging to straps, jerking them up elevator shafts and pouring them on to the ferry-boats. But this accidental great thing is at times a very great thing. . . .

*　*　*

I corrected that first crowded impression of New York with a clearer, brighter vision of expansiveness when next day I began to realise the social quality of New York's central backbone, between Fourth Avenue and Sixth. The effect remained still that of an immeasurably powerful forward movement of rapid eager advance, a process of enlargement and increment in every material sense. . . . It grew upon me that the Twentieth Century, which found New York brownstone of the color of desiccated chocolate, meant to leave it a city of white and colored marble. I found myself agape, admiring a skyscraper—the prow of the Flat-Iron Building, to be particular, ploughing up through the traffic of Broadway and Fifth Avenue in the afternoon light. The New York sundown and twilight seemed to me quite glorious things. Down the western streets one gets the sky hung in long cloud-barred strips like Japanese paintings, celestial tranquil yellows and greens and pink luminosity toning down to the reeking blue-brown edge of the distant New Jersey atmosphere, and the clear black hard activity of crowd and trolley-car and Elevated railroad. Against this deepening color came the innumerable little lights of the house cliffs and the street tier above tier. New York is lavish of light, it is lavish of everything, it is full of the sense of spending from an inexhaustible supply. For a time one is drawn irresistibly into the universal belief in that inexhaustible supply.

H. G. Wells
The Future in America

The Power and Motion of the City

After an absence, I am now again (September, 1870) in New York city and Brooklyn, on a few weeks' vacation. The splendor, picturesqueness, and oceanic amplitude and rush of these great cities, the unsurpass'd situation, rivers and bay, sparkling sea-tides, costly and lofty new buildings, facades of marble and iron, of original grandeur and elegance of design, with the masses of gay color, the preponderance of white and blue, the flags flying, the endless ships, the tumultuous streets, Broadway, the heavy, low, musical roar, hardly ever intermitted, even at night; the jobbers' houses, the rich shops, the wharves, the great Central Park, and the Brooklyn Park of hills, (as I wander among them this beautiful fall weather, musing, watching, absorbing)—the assemblages of the citizens in their groups, conversations, trades, evening amusements, or along the by-quarters— these, I say, and the like of these, completely satisfy my senses of power, fulness, motion, etc., and give me, through such senses and appetites, and through my esthetic conscience, a continued exaltation and absolute fulfilment. Always and more and more, as I cross the East and North rivers, the ferries, or with the pilots in their pilot-houses, or pass an hour in Wall street, or the gold exchange, I realize, (if we must admit such partialisms,) that not Nature alone is great in her fields of freedom and the open air, in her storms, the shows of night and day, the mountains, forests, seas—but in the artificial, the work of man too is equally great—in this profusion of teeming humanity—in these ingenuities, streets, goods, houses, ships—these hurrying, feverish, electric crowds of men, their complicated business genius, (not least among the geniuses,) and all this mighty, many-threaded wealth and industry concentrated here.

Walt Whitman
Democratic Vistas

Manhattan is like a Poem

A poem compresses much in a small space and adds music, thus heightening its meaning. The city is like poetry: it compresses all life, all races and breeds, into a small island and adds music and the accompaniment of internal engines. The island of Manhattan is without any doubt the greatest human concentrate on earth, the poem whose magic is comprehensible to millions of permanent residents but whose full meaning will always remain elusive. At the feet of the tallest and plushiest offices lie the crummiest slums. The genteel mysteries housed in the Riverside Church are only a few blocks from the voodoo charms of Harlem. The merchant princes, riding to Wall Street in their limousines down the East River Drive, pass within a few hundred yards of the gypsy kings; but the princes do not know they are passing kings, and the kings are not up yet anyway—they live a more leisurely life than the princes and get drunk more consistently.

New York is nothing like Paris; it is nothing like London; and it is not Spokane multiplied by sixty, or Detroit multiplied by four. It is by all odds the loftiest of cities. It even managed to reach the highest point in the sky at the lowest moment of the depression. The Empire State Building shot twelve hundred and fifty feet into the air when it was madness to put out as much as six inches of new growth. . . .

Manhattan has been compelled to expand sky-ward because of the absence of any other direction in which to grow. This, more than any other thing, is responsible for its physical majesty. It is to the nation what the white church spire is to the village—the visible symbol of aspiration and faith, the white plume saying that the way is up. The summer traveler swings in over Hell Gate Bridge and from the window of his sleeping car as it glides above the pigeon lofts and back yards of Queens looks southwest to where the morning light first strikes the steel peaks of midtown, and he sees its upward thrust unmistakable: the great walls and towers rising, the smoke rising, the heat not yet rising, the hopes and ferments of so many awakening millions rising—this vigorous spear that presses heaven hard.

E. B. White
Here is New York

82

4. The Noble Bridges

The Supreme American Achievement

Of all the devices by which the New Yorkers have assuaged their restless urges, much the most splendid are the bridges. I agree with V. S. Pritchett who says in his *New York Proclaimed* that these are the finest things the New Yorker has ever made—"architecturally it is the bridges rather than the buildings or even the way of life that are the supreme American achievement." For the lover of bridges, this is the ultimate city. If Venice and Amsterdam have more, if San Francisco possesses one arguably more thrilling, if Isfahan and Florence have more peculiar examples, if Sydney is more theatrically dominated by a single bridge, and Paris more absolutely by a dozen, still New York is richer in noble bridges than any other city in the world.

This is a gift of the archipelago. Bridges are everywhere around this Bay, their towers and latticeworks looming at the ends of streets, their suspension wires foreshortened by perspective so that the three East River bridges sometimes seem to be all in a tangle of steel wire and stanchion. Over Newark Bay the hump-back of the Bayonne Bridge stands in massive silhouette, and far up towards Long Island Sound the towers of the suspension bridges are scattered inexplicably across the landscape, in places where no water seems to be. . . .

Sometimes I walked across Brooklyn Bridge, if the morning was fine enough, and I was in a bridge mood. There is a boardwalk across it, in the center of the span, and there the pedestrian has a breezy sense of supremacy, as he strides across the planking in the morning sun, the cars out of sight below him, and silenced by the wind, the East River opening away into the grand expanse of the upper bay. . . . It caught the imagination of the world from the start, and its origins were made romantic by tragedy: its designer, the German, John Roebling, was injured by a ferryboat during the work and died of tetanus; his son Washington, who took over, collapsed while working in a pneumatic caisson, and was paralyzed for life. The bridge was opened in 1883, the celebratory parade making a detour to Roebling's house to pay tribute to the invalid engineer. It remained for twenty years the longest suspension bridge in the world.

J. H. Morris
The Great Port

The Bridge

What bridge?
Great God, the only bridge,
The bridge of power, life and joy,
The bridge that was a span, a cry, an ecstasy—
That was America.

What bridge?
The bridge whose wing-like sweep
Like space and joy and ecstasy
Was mixed like music in his blood,
Would beat like flight and joy and triumph
Through the conduits of his life forever.

What bridge?
The bridge whereon at night he had walked
And stood and watched, a thousand times,
Until every fabric of its soaring web
Was inwrought in his memory,
And every living sinew of its million cabled nerves
Had throbbed and pulsed in his own spirit
Like his soul's anatomy.

"The—the Brooklyn Bridge," he mumbled.
"The—the Bridge is good."

Thomas Wolfe

A Walk Across the Brooklyn Bridge

One fresh November morning—Indian summer prolongs the fine, sunny days up to the threshold of the new year—I had myself driven to the far end of the Brooklyn Bridge, on the left bank of the East River, and I returned to Manhattan on foot, over the bridge. It is a long distance on the foot walk and you are surrounded or dominated by the lanes for elevateds and cars. The sky before you bristles with the skyscrapers of Wall Street; they are rose-colored, gay, in the maritime sky. They are shaggy, crowned with gold or debatable architectural ornament. A violent feeling takes hold of you: the feeling of unanimity. There should be sensations of contriteness, of troubled judgement and taste, reservations, doubt, cacophony. But no! There is a dominating force: unity; a subjugating element: magnitude.

Yes! let us recognize that America has given us that sensation: magnitude which is noble, which can be very noble, as it often was in the past. Imagine the white cathedrals in an incompletely finished world, erect, straight, above the small houses. We have no right to inveigh against magnitude. Nor do we have the right to fall back on an egoism based on laziness and invoke "measure." We did not come to the USA to look for measure, but to look for conviction and enthusiasm.

Our European wearinesses require a tonic. I can hear the traitors, the defeatists, the sanctimonious people in France; later on I shall speak of a French professor who came to New York University to fulfill a sacred mission(!). "I try to teach them good taste and measure." You do not walk into a battlefield or into one of the vast workshops of the world in dress clothes and patent leather shoes, mouthing discourses. Too many complacent people do nothing but carp and talk like Pompadours to sweating nations caught in the tentacles of the struggle for life.

Brooklyn Bridge, which is old (elevateds, cars, trucks, pedestrians all have special lanes), is as strong and rugged as a gladiator, while George Washington Bridge, built yesterday, smiles like a young athlete. In this case the two large Gothic towers of stone are very handsome because they are American and not "Beaux-Arts." They are full of native sap and they are not graceful, but strong. The vertical cables are black and not silver, but in perspective their vertical fall fixes a spidery veil. It is an imposing architectural sensation; vertical, slender, immense, yes, I come back to the immense and like a barbarian I enjoy it, or better, as a man animated by a constructive spirit, active but wearied by the depressing atmosphere of cowardice and abdication in Paris, crushed, often dishonored, treated as a madman and Utopian, consigned to the Greek calends, etc. . . . here I find reality. And it brings me a profound satisfaction.

Reality, that is the lesson of America. It gives our boldest speculation the certainty of imminent birth.

Le Corbusier
When the Cathedrals Were White

The Quest of the Fair Medusa

George took Randy's advice and moved. He did not know where to go. All he wanted was to get away as far as possible from Park Avenue, from the aesthetic jungles of the lion hunters, from the half-life of wealth and fashion that had grown like a parasite upon the sound body of America. He went to live in Brooklyn.

He had made a little money from his book, so now he paid his debts and quit the job he held as a teacher at the School for Utility Cultures. From this time on, he earned his precarious living solely by what he wrote.

For four years he lived in Brooklyn, and four years in Brooklyn are a geologic age—a single stratum of grey time. They were years of poverty, of desperation, of loneliness unutterable. All about him were the poor, the outcast, the neglected and forsaken people of America, and he was one of them. But life is strong, and year after year it went on around him in all its manifold complexity, rich with its unnoticed and unrecorded little happenings. He saw it all, he took it all in hungrily as part of his experience, he recorded much of it, and in the end he squeezed it dry as he tried to extract its hidden meanings.

And what was he like inside while these grey years were slipping by? What was he up to, what was he doing, what did he want?

That's rather hard to tell, because he wanted so many things, but the thing he wanted most was Fame. Those were the years of his concentrated quest of that fair Medusa. He had had his little taste of glory, and it was bitter in his mouth. He thought the reason was that he had not been good enough—and he had not been good enough. Therefore he thought that what he had had was not Fame at all, but only a moment's notoriety. He had been a seven-day wonder—that was all.

Well, he had learned some things since he wrote his first book. He would try again.

So he lived and wrote, and wrote and lived, and lived there by himself in Brooklyn. And when he had worked for hours at a stretch, forgetting food and sleep and everything, he would rise from his desk at last and stagger forth into the nighttime streets, reeling like a drunkard with his weariness. He would eat his supper at a restaurant, and then, because his mind was feverish and he knew he could not sleep, he would walk to Brooklyn Bridge and cross it to Manhattan, and ferret out the secret heart of darkness in all the city's ways, and then at dawn come back across the Bridge once more, and so to bed in Brooklyn.

And in these nightly wanderings the old refusals dropped away, the old avowals stood. For then, somehow, it seemed to him that he who had been dead was risen, he who had been lost was found again, and he who in his brief day of glory had sold the talent, the passion, and the belief of his youth into the keeping of the fleshless dead, until his heart was corrupted and all hope gone, would win his life back bloodily, in solitude and darkness. And he felt then that things would be for him once more as they had been, and he saw again, as he had once seen, the image of the shining city. Far-flung, and blazing into tiers of jeweled light, it burned forever in his vision as he walked the Bridge, and strong tides were bound around it, and the great ships called. So he walked the Bridge, always he walked the Bridge.

And by his side was that stern friend, the only one to whom he spoke what in his secret heart he most desired. To Loneliness he whispered, "Fame!"—and Loneliness replied, "Aye, brother, wait and see."

Thomas Wolfe
You Can't Go Home Again

To Brooklyn Bridge

How many dawns, chill from his rippling rest
The seagull's wings shall dip and pivot him,
Shedding white rings of tumult, building high
Over the chained bay waters Liberty—

Then, with inviolate curve, forsake our eyes
As apparitional as sails that cross
Some page of figures to be filed away;
—Till elevators drop us from our day . . .

I think of cinemas, panoramic sleights
With multitudes bent toward some flashing scene
Never disclosed, but hastened to again,
Foretold to other eyes on the same screen;

And Thee, across the harbor, silver-paced
As though the sun took step of thee, yet left
Some motion ever unspent in thy stride,—
Implicitly they freedom staying thee!

Out of some subway scuttle, cell or loft
A bedlamite speeds to thy parapets,
Tilting there momently, shrill shirt ballooning,
A jest falls from the speechless caravan.

Down Wall, from girder into street noon leaks,
A rip-tooth of the sky's acetylene;
All afternoon the cloud-flown derricks turn . . .
Thy cables breathe the North Atlantic still.

And obscure as that heaven of the Jews,
Thy guerdon . . . Accolade thou dost bestow
Of anonymity time cannot raise:
Vibrant reprieve and pardon thou dost show.

O harp and altar, of the fury fused,
(How could mere toil align thy choiring strings!)
Terrific threshold of the prophet's pledge,
Prayer of pariah, and the lover's cry,—

Again the traffic lights that skim thy swift
Unfractioned idiom, immaculate sigh of stars,
Beading thy path—condense eternity:
And we have seen night lifted in thine arms.

Under thy shadow by the piers I waited;
Only in darkness is thy shadow clear.
The City's fiery parcels all undone,
Already snow submerges an iron year . . .

O Sleepless as the river under thee,
Vaulting the sea, the prairies' dreaming sod,
Unto us lowliest sometime sweep, descend
And of the curveship lend a myth to God.

Hart Crane

The Bridge Builder

An old man, going a lone highway,
Came at the evening, cold and gray,
To a chasm, vast and deep and wide,
Through which was flowing a sullen tide.
The old man crossed in the twilight dim—
That sullen stream had no fears for him;
But he turned, when he reached the other side,
And built a bridge to span the tide.

"Old man," said a fellow pilgrim near,
"You are wasting strength in building here.
Your journey will end with the ending day;
You never again must pass this way.
You have crossed the chasm, deep and wide,
Why build you the bridge at the eventide?"

The builder lifted his old gray head.
"Good friend, in the path I have come," he said,
"There followeth after me today
A youth whose feet must pass this way.
This chasm that has been naught to me
To that fair-haired youth may a pitfall be.
He, too, must cross in the twilight dim;
Good friend, I am building the bridge for *him*."

Will Allen Dromgoole

The George Washington Bridge: A Place of Radiant Grace

At the opposite end of the city—Wall Street being at the South end of Manhattan—at the northern extremity of the island, the George Washington Bridge spans the Hudson—an arm of the sea or an estuary rather than a river. The floor of the bridge, as in other bridges, is high enough to allow the passage of large ships. Thus the approaches have to be carefully designed ramps which gradually dominate the city. American bridges are of the suspension type. That expresses a trait of mind. What are bridges for? To enable you to cross over on a horizontal platform, but also to allow a free space below for the passage of boats: that principle is accepted everywhere. Monumental arches? They are not in question, it is a question of a bridge! Daring is a virtue, and, assisted by technique, it has made possible at certain happy moments the attainment of architectural splendor.

The George Washington Bridge over the Hudson is the most beautiful bridge in the world. Made of cables and steel beams, it gleams in the sky like a reversed arch. It is blessed. It is the only seat of grace in the disordered city. It is painted an aluminum color and, between water and sky, you see nothing but the bent cord supported by two steel towers. When your car moves up the ramp the two towers rise so high that it brings you happiness; their structure is so pure, so resolute, so regular that here, finally, steel architecture seems to laugh. The car reaches an unexpectedly wide apron; the second tower is very far away; innumerable vertical cables, gleaming against the sky, are suspended from the magisterial curve which swings down and then up. The rose-colored towers of New York appear, a vision whose harshness is mitigated by distance.

The bridge has a story which almost turned out ridiculously. Mr. Cullman, president of the Port of New York, told me about it. The bridge was constructed under his supervision. The problem required the utmost engineering boldness. Calculation aided by a fortunate hypothesis gave the work the severity of things which are exact. The bridge leaps over the Hudson in a single bound. Two steel-topped concrete piers between the banks and the apron hold the suspension chains. I have mentioned the extraordinary dimensions of the two towers. Constructed of riveted steel they stand up in the sky with a striking nobility. Now the towers were to have been faced with stone molded and sculptured in "Beaux-Arts" style (New York term for the aesthetic ideas current on the quai Voltaire in Paris).

Someone acted before it was too late. Then the whole committee of the Port of New York Authority. Little by little the spirit of modern times makes itself felt: these men said, "Stop! no stone or decoration here. The two towers and the mathematical play of the cables make a splendid unity. It is one. That is the new beauty."

Le Corbusier
When the Cathedrals Were White

116

5. The Ships

After the Sea Ship

After the Sea-Ship—after the whistling winds;
After the white-gray sails, taut to their spars
        and ropes.
Below, a myriad, myriad waves, hastening, lifting up their
        necks,
Tending in ceaseless flow
        toward the track of the ship:
Waves of the ocean, bubbling and gurgling,
        blithely prying,
Waves, undulating waves—liquid, uneven, emulous waves,
Toward that whirling current, laughing and buoyant, with
        curves
Where the great Vessel, sailing and tacking, displaced the
        surface;
Larger and smaller waves,
        in the spread of the ocean,
        yearnfully flowing;
The wake of the Sea-Ship, after she passes—flashing and
        frolicsome, under the sun,
A motley procession, with many a fleck of foam, and many
        fragments,
Following the stately and rapid Ship—in the wake following.

                              Walt Whitman

Luck

What bring you sailor, home from the sea—
  Coffers of gold and of ivory?

When first I went to sea as a lad
  A new jackknife was all I had;

And I've sailed for fifty years and three
  To the coasts of gold and of ivory;

And now at the end of a lucky life,
  Well, still I've got my old jackknife.

Wilfrid Gibson

A Sea Song From the Shore

HAIL! Ho!
Sail! Ho!
Ahoy! Ahoy! Ahoy!
Who calls to me,
So far at sea?
Only a little boy!

Sail! Ho!
Hail! Ho!
The sailor he sails the sea:
I wish he would capture
a little sea-horse
And send him home to me.

I wish, as he sails
Through the tropical gales,
He would catch me a sea-bird, too,
With its silver wings
And the song it sings,
And its breast of down and dew!

James Whitcomb Riley

The Ship

For men are wise:
They know that they are lost,
They know that they are desolate and damned together;
They look out upon the tumult of unending water,
And they know there is no answer,
And that the sea,
The sea, is its own end and answer.
Then they lay paths across it,
They make harbors at the end,
And log their courses to them,
They believe in earth and go to find it,
They launch great ships,
They put a purpose down upon the purposeless waste.

And this ship was the latest of them all
Upon the timeless seas.
She set a day, and fixed a mark on history.
She was the child of all other ships
That had made their dots of time
And that had brought small, vivid men and all their history
Upon the water—The Greeks, and the Phoenician traders,
The wild, blond Norsemen with their plaited hair,
The hot Spaniards, the powdered Frenchmen with their wigs,
And the bluff English, moving in to close and board and conquer.

These men were lords and captains on the sea,
And they had given mortal tongue, and
Meters of mortal time, to timelessness.
Yes! they made strong clocks
Strike sweetly out upon the ocean;
They took the timeless, yearless sea
And put the measure of their years upon it;
They said, "In such-and-such a year we made this sea our own
And took her for our ship and country."

This was the ship,
And she was time and life there on the ocean. If from sea-caves cold
The ageless monsters of the deep had risen,
The polyped squirm and women with no loins and seaweed hair,
They could have read her time and destiny,
She cared for none of this,
For she was healthy with the life of man,
And men care little for the sea-cave cold.
In their few million years, what do they know
Of the vast swarming kingdoms of the sea, or of the earth
Beyond their scratchings on it?

Thomas Wolfe

Song for All Seas, All Ships

1

To-Day a rude brief recitative,
Of ships sailing the Seas, each with its special flag or ship-
    signal;
Of unnamed heroes in the ships—Of waves spreading and
    spreading, far as the eye can reach;
Of dashing spray, and the winds piping and blowing;
And out of these a chant, for the sailors of all nations,
Fitful, like a surge.

Of Sea-Captains young or old, and the Mates—and of all in-
    trepid Sailors;
Of the few, very choice, taciturn, whom fate can never surprise,
    nor death dismay,
Pick'd sparingly, without noise, by thee, old Ocean—chosen by
    thee,
Thou Sea, that pickest and cullest the race, in Time, and unitest
    Nations!
Suckled by thee, old husky Nurse—embodying thee!
Indomitable, untamed as thee.

(Ever the heroes, on water or on land, by ones or twos
    appearing,
Ever the stock preserv'd, and never lost, though rare—enough
    for seed preserv'd.)

2

Flaunt out O Sea, your separate flags of nations!
Flaunt out, visible as ever, the various ship-signals!
But do you reserve especially for yourself, and for the soul of
    man, one flag above all the rest,
A spiritual woven Signal, for all nations, emblem of man elate
    above death,
Token of all brave captains, and all intrepid sailors and mates,
And all that went down doing their duty;
Reminiscent of them—twined from all intrepid captains, young
    or old;
A pennant universal, subtly waving, all time, o'er all brave
    sailors,
All seas, all ships.

Walt Whitman

Sailing Day Scenes:
On The Dock Of A Big Ocean Liner—
Just Before The Start

The interior of the huge pier had been long thronged with trucks, merchandise and people. A great babble of voices and roar of wheels arose from it. Over all rang the wild incoherent shouts of the bosses, who directed the stevedores. These latter marched in endless procession, with bales and bags upon their shoulders. It was the last of the cargo. They ferreted their way stolidly through the noisy crowds of visitors and then up a wide gangplank in steady and monotonous procession.

Through the wide doors in the side of the pier could be seen the mighty sides of the steamer, and above little stretches of white deck, whereon people stood in rows gazing fixedly at the shore as if they expected at any moment to see it vanish. At the end of the passenger gangplank two sailors remained imperturbably at their station. An officer leaned on the railing near them. Near the shoreward end swarmed countless stewards, mingling their blue uniforms in with the gay colored clothes of the crowd and wondering assiduously about everybody's business.

From a position near the doors one could see that the enormous funnels of the steamship were emitting continual streams of black, curling smoke.

Gradually there was a vanishing of the stewards. The two sailors at the gangplank began to look serious and rather wild, as if the responsibility of their positions and the eye of the adjacent officer was too much for them. Rows of stevedores manned ropes and prepared to tug at the gangplanks. Meanwhile, from all along the line of the pier, extraordinary conversations were being held with people who leaned upon the railings of the decks above. A preliminary thrill went through the throng. The talk began to grow hurried, excited. People spoke wildly and with great speed, conscious that the last moments were upon them. And it devolved upon certain individuals to lose their friends at the final minute in the chaos of heads upon the decks, so that one could often hear the same typical formula coming from a dozen different sources, as if everybody was interested in the same person and had missed him. Two grayheaded New Yorkers held a frantic argument.

"There he is! There he is! Hurray! Goodby, ol' man!"

"Darn it all, I tell you that it isn't him at all!"

"It is, too!"

"It ain't, I tell you!"

"Ah, there he is now. Down there further! Goodby, ol' man, goodby!"

A man upon the steamer suddenly burst out in a fury of gesticulation. "Where's Tommie?" he bawled. "I can't see Tommie!"

His excitement was communicated to two women upon the pier. "Heavens!" said one with a nervous cry, "Where is that boy!" She could not omit some complainings of motherhood. "He's the greatest plague! Here's his father sailing for Europe and he's off somewhere! Tommie! Tommie! Come here!" They began to glance frenziedly through the crevices of the crowd. It was plain that they expected to detect him in some terrible, irrelevant crime.

Then suddenly above the clamor of farewells arose the wild shout of a little boy, undismayed by the crowds. "Papa! Papa! Papa! Here I am! Goodby, papa!" The man on the steamship made a tremendous gesture. The two women on the pier began to weep vaguely.

The faces on all sides beamed with affection and some sort of a suggestion of mournful reminiscence. There were plentiful smiles, but they expressed always a great tender sorrow. It was surprising to see how full of expression the face of a blunt, every day American business man could become. They were suddenly angels.

As for the women, they were sacred from stare through the purity of their grief. Many of them allowed the tears to fall unheeded down their faces. Theirs was a quality of sorrow that has a certain valor, a certain boldness.

The crowd began to swarm toward the end of the pier to get the last gesture and glance of their friends as the steamer backed out. It was coming toward the supreme moment.

At last some indefinite mechanism set the sailors and the stevedores in motion. Ropes were flung away and the heavy gangplanks were pulled back onto the dock with loud shouts. "Look out! Look out there!" The people were unheeding, for now uprose a great tumult of farewells, a song of affection that swelled into a vast incoherent roar. They had waited long for this moment, and now with a sense of its briefness they were frantic in an effort to think how best to use it. Handkerchiefs waved in white clouds. Men bawled in a last futile struggle to express their state of mind. Over all could often be heard the shrill wail of the little boy! "Oh, papa! Papa! Here I am!" . . .

Out at the end of the pier the whole final uproar was in full motion. A tug loaded with gesturing, howling people bustled to and fro, celebrating everything with a barbaric whistle. A last great cry arose as steel hued water began to show between the craft and the pier. It was a farewell with an undercurrent of despair of expression. The inadequacy of the goodbys seemed suddenly apparent to the crowd. The forlorn pathos of the thing struck their minds anew and many of the women began to weep again in that vague way, as if overcome by a sadness that was subtly more than the tangible grief of parting.

Stephen Crane
New York City Sketches

At Sea

YEA, we go down to sea in ships—
    But Hope remains behind,
And Love, with laughter on his lips,
    And Peace, of passive mind;
While out across the deeps of night,
    With lifted sails of prayer,
We voyage off in quest of light,
    Nor find it anywhere.

O Thou who wroughtest earth and sea,
    Yet keepest from our eyes
The shores of an eternity
    In calms of Paradise,
Blow back upon our foolish quest
    With all the driving rain
Of blinding tears and wild unrest,
    And waft us home again!

James Whitcomb Riley

Manhattan's Dear Isle

'Tis the evening of Christmas, the maskers have met,
And the dark eyes of Lima are moisten'd with glee;
The harp of Peru and the wild castinet,
Are mingled together in sweet minstrelsy.
Our messmates have left us to join in the throng,
Yet tho' quite alone, Tom, the time we'll beguile,
For our hearts are attuned to the beauty and song
Of the maidens that dwell in Manhattan's dear Isle.

Over many a league of the perilous main
We have wandered together in moonlight and storm,
And we've mused in our watch of the smiles that again
Would welcome us back, and our eager hearts warm.
In the valleys of Chili there's many an eye
Whose eloquent gaze has enslaved us awhile;
But oh, from the depths of our spirits a sigh
Speeds over the sea to Manhattan's dear Isle.

The sleigh bells are chiming and merry cheeks glow
With the keen blast of winter, and tho'ts of delight;
The moon, in her beauty, illumines the snow,
And loved tones are breathed round our hearthstone tonight;
Oh! would we were present those moments to share,
To meet from our kindred affection's dear smile,
To linger again near those beings so fair,
With the maidens that dwell in Manhattan's dear Isle.

Oh! years have gone by since the anchor was weighed,
And the voices we love, bade a kindly "good-bye;"
Since the Highlands grew dim in the eventide shade,
And we stood to the East, 'neath a bright autumn sky;
But soon thro' the turbulent gales of Cape Horn,
Our long absent vessel will struggle awhile,
Until from the land of the stranger she's borne,
And anchors once more near Manhattan's dear Isle.

Midshipman W. F. Spicer U.S.N.
Christmas Night, 1843
U.S.S. Relief–Callao, Peru

The Hooker

As good a place as any to get the feel of the port is the office of the Kennedy Towing Line at 32 South Street. It is the last old-fashioned tugboat office left. The bigger lines have gone down to buildings like 24 State and 17 Battery Place, where they employ female stenographers and rub elbows with transatlantic steamship companies. But a potbellied iron stove still overheats the Kennedy office from early fall until late spring, and a gay blue and white portrait of the tug *Idlewild*, with more paint than perspective, provides its chief adornment. Of the six Kennedy boats two were built before 1875. It is Tom Wilson's favorite office for yarning.

Tom is the senior tugboat master of the harbor, with a voice on him like the Staten Island Ferry boat and a chest like an oil drum.

"I am seventy-four years old," he roars, "and I can jump out of that window and jump right back again." The office is on the second floor. "When they put me together they put me together right," says Tom, heaving on a handful of snow white hair. "Every hair drove in with a nail. None of your shin plasters.

"I went tug-boatin' when I was eighteen, aboard of the *Leonard Richards*, the twin of that *Idlewild* in the pitcher. Where did I go to sea from? The First Ward. Tugboat captains was the cream of society in them days. They wore high hats and gold watch chains and Prince Albert coats and striped trousers, and they never touched the wheel without kid gloves. They would steal the sight out of your eyes.

"The *Leonard Richards* was a Hooker. What was a Hooker? Why, a tug that cruised off Sandy Hook for schooners, of course. Just the same as a Gater was a tug that hanged off Hell Gate, and a Lugger was a tug that lugged ships to their berths after the Hookers and the Gaters brought them in, whether the ships was pine wooders from the South, or brickers, or whatever they might be.

"Them days there was more ships than now, and plenty of sail. The most part of them had no regular agents ashore to hire tugs, and there was no radio, anyway, so the agents wouldn't a 'knowed when they was coming in. The first tug that seed a ship he made up to her and the two captains paced their deck awhile and called each other this and that and at last they struck a bargain, or they didn't, and you sheered off and he run up the American flag for another tug.

"But the tug that got out first had the best chance. So sometimes at night the captain would shake you by the shoulder and say, 'Get up and cast off with no noise,' and you would try to give the other boats the shake and get out to sea before they was wise. You would go out without lights, by Rockaway or South Beach or Coney Island, where you knowed there was nothing you could hit only maybe an oyster boat, and you wouldn't stop for that.

"Sometimes when you would get out in the stream you would hear the whistles tooting if they suspicioned you, and the whole gang would be after you.

"Then, if the old man was wise, he would switch his running lights. He would put his red and green lights astern and his white light on the bow, and it would look like he was coming in instead of going out . . . .

"Thirty or forty hours at a stretch working was nothing. The first command I got, after I got my license in 1883, I asked my owner for some bedding so's the men could lay down. 'I didn't hire them men to sleep,' he says. I can work thirty hours right now without squealing, and on my hoofs, too.

"Then when you would get out there sometimes there would be a good wind and they would sail right past you, and maybe offer you a line.

"But when the wind died they had a different tune.

"Once I picked up a French bark off Fire Island, and I couldn't make a price with him. I follied him and I follied him, and at Long Beach, sure enough he goes ashore. Now I had him, I figured, and he would pay me a damn good price to pull him off. Up comes a nor'west gale, and what does the sucker do but back her off under sail! Ah, well, heartaches in every trade.

"But one time they wouldn't bargain was the war. That was the golden age. All I had to do was cruise down by the Highlands on a calm day and take my pick of the schooners and barks that was bringing supplies to New York. I would make up to the one that looked the best bet.

" 'Morning, Captain,' I would tell the old man. 'Seed anything of a submarine around here?'

" 'My god!' he would say. 'So close to New York?'

" 'Shelled a ship up by Hoffman's Island this morning,' I would say.

" 'How much to take me in?'

" 'Fifteen hundred dollars.'

" 'You're a pirate. I'll not pay it.'

" 'Very good, Captain. Sorry we can't do business, Captain. But I ain't got no time to waste out here. I don't want to lose this little craft or the few lives I got on board.'

"I'd start off, and five minutes later he'd be signaling for me to come back and tow him at my price.

"When I'd get him up to Quarantine I'd drop him. 'If you want to go any further,' I'd say, 'get a local. This is an express.' "

A. J. Liebling
Back Where I Came From

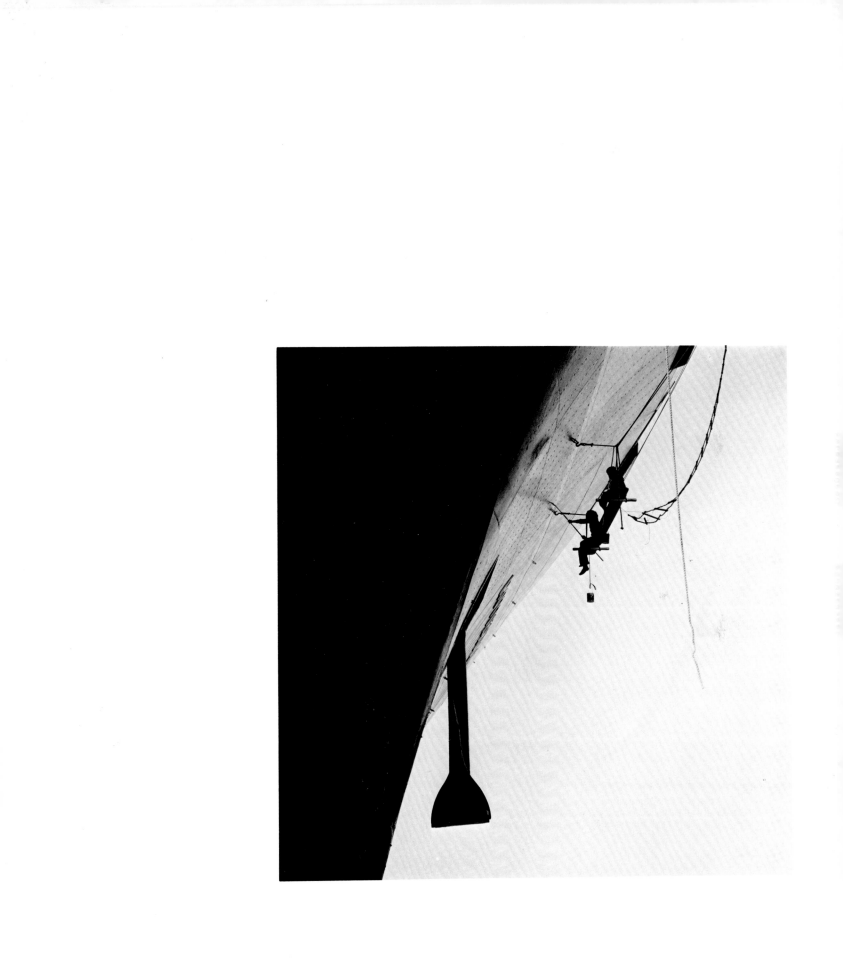

6. Around New York

The Desert Isle

Do you realize that one can't look in
any direction in Manhattan without seeing
water at the end of the street: the Harbor,
the Hudson and East Rivers, the Narrows,
and even the Atlantic. Here we are entering
the age of Aquarius, the age of water, with
New York the wateriest city in the entire
world. Yet we, who could be beachcombers on
a dozen exciting waterfronts, live here as if
we were in the middle of the Sahara!

Helen Hayes,
Anita Loos
Twice Over Lightly

City Streets

There is no spot of country green more beautiful
    to me
Than old Manhattan's genial streets, without a
    rose or tree,
For people dwell within these streets, with human
    hearts like mine.
And toil and dreaming, tears and smiles, are after
    all, divine.

The fragrant hills in springtime are pleasant ways
    to roam,
But I am always happiest when in my city home,
Where every street is like a scene in some romantic
    play,
And every man and woman, child, an actor—
    sad or gay.

I do not envy him who longs for forest,
    sea and sail,
From boyhood days, the streets have sung to me
    their wonder tale;
It is a tale of people, not a song of stream and dell,
And so I love the city streets, where human beings
    dwell.

Morris Abel Beer

Dusk

Dusk gently smooths crispangled streets.
Dark presses tight the steaming asphalt city,
crushes the fretwork of windows and lettered
signs and chimneys and watertanks and
ventilators and fire-escapes and moldings and
patterns and corrugations and eyes and hands
and neckties into blue chunks, into black
enormous blocks. Under the rolling heavier
heavier pressure windows blurt light.
Night crushes bright milk out of arclights,
squeezes the sullen blocks until they drip red,
yellow, green into streets resounding with feet.
All the asphalt oozes light. Light spurts from
lettering on roofs, mills dizzily among wheels,
stains rolling tons of sky.

John Dos Passos
Manhattan Transfer

Vision of the City

It was a cruel city, but it was a lovely one;
A savage city, yet it had such tenderness;
A bitter, harsh, and violent catacomb of stone and steel
 and tunneled rock,
Slashed savagely with light,
And roaring, fighting a constant ceaseless warfare of
 men and of machinery;
And yet it was so sweetly and so delicately pulsed,
As full of warmth, of passion, and of love,
As it was full of hate.

And even the very skies that framed New York,
The texture of the night itself,
Seemed to have the architecture and the weather
Of the city's special quality.

It was, he saw, a Northern city:
The bases of its form were vertical.
Even the night here, the quality of darkness,
Had a structural framework, and architecture of its own.
Here, compared with qualities of night
In London or in Paris,
Which were rounder, softer, of more drowsy hue,
The night was vertical, lean, immensely clifflike, steep
 and clear.
Here everything was sharp.
It burned so brightly, yet it burned sweetly, too.

For what was so incredible and so lovely
About this high, cool night
Was that it could be so harsh and clear,
So arrogantly formidable, and yet so tender, too.

There were always in these nights, somehow,
Even in nights of clear and bitter cold,
Not only the structure of lean steel,
But a touch of April, too:
They could be insolent and cruel,
And yet there was always in them
The suggestion of light feet, of lilac darkness,
Of something swift and fleeting,
Almost captured, ever gone,
A maiden virginal as April.

Here in this sky-hung faëry of the night,
The lights were sown like flung stars.
Suddenly he got a vision of the city
That was overwhelming in its loveliness.
It seemed to him all at once that there was nothing there
But the enchanted architecture of the dark,
Star-sown with a million lights.
He forgot the buildings:
All of a sudden, the buildings did not seem to exist,
To be there at all.
Darkness itself seemed to provide the structure
For the star-dust of those million lights,
They were flung there against the robe of night
Like jewels spangled on the gown of the dark Helen
That is burning in man's blood forevermore.

And the magic of it was incredible.
Light blazed before him, soared above him, mounted
        in linkless chains,
Was sown there upon a viewless wall, soared to the
        very pinnacles of night,
Inwrought into the robe of dark itself,
Unbodied, unsustained,
Yet fixed and moveless as a changeless masonry,
A world of darkness, the invisible,
Lighted for some immortal feast.

                                        Thomas Wolfe

Night Movement—New York

In the night, when the sea-winds take the city in their arms,
And cool the loud streets that kept their dust noon and afternoon;
In the night, when the sea-birds call to the lights of the city,
The lights that cut on the skyline their name of a city;
In the night, when the trains and wagons start from a long way off
For the city where the people ask bread and want letters;
In the night the city lives too—the day is not all.
In the night there are dancers dancing and singers singing,
And the sailors and soldiers look for numbers on doors.
In the night the sea-winds take the city in their arms.

                                        Carl Sandburg

7. Solitude by the Water

Hymn of The City

Not in the solitude
Alone may man commune with Heaven, or see,
Only in savage wood
And sunny vale, the present Deity;
Or hear his voice
Where the winds whisper and the waves rejoice.

Even here do I behold
Thy steps, Almighty!—here, amidst the crowd
Through the great city rolled,
With everlasting murmur deep and loud—
Choking the ways that wind
'Mongst the proud piles, the work of human kind.

Thy golden sunshine comes
From the round heaven, and on their dwellings lies
And lights their inner homes;
For them thou fill'st with air the unbounded skies,
And givest them the stores
Of ocean, and the harvests of its shores.

William Cullen Bryant

A Scene on the Banks of the Hudson

Cool shades and dews are round my way,
And silence of the early day;
Mid the dark rocks that watch his bed
Glitters the mighty Hudson spread,
Unrippled, save by drops that fall
From shrubs that fringe his mountain wall;
And o'er the clear still water swells
The music of the Sabbath bells.

All, save this little nook of land,
Circled with trees on which I stand;
All, save that line of hills which lie
Suspended in the mimic sky—
Seems a blue void, above, below,
Through which the white clouds come and go;
And from the green world's farthest steep
I gaze into the airy deep.

Loveliest of lovely things are they,
On earth, that soonest pass away.
The rose that lives its little hour
Is prized beyond the sculptured flower.
Even love, long tried and cherished long,
Becomes more tender and more strong
At thought of that insatiate grave
From which its yearnings cannot save.

River! in this still hour thou hast
Too much of heaven on earth to last;
Nor long may thy still waters lie,
An image of the glorious sky.
Thy fate and mine are not repose,
And ere another evening close,
Thou to thy tides shalt turn again,
And I to seek the crowd of men.

William Cullen Bryant

The Hudson

'Twas a vision of childhood that came with its
    dawn,
Ere the curtain that covered life's day-star was
    drawn;
The nurse told the tale when the shadows grew long,
And the mother's soft lullaby breathed it in song.

"There flows a fair stream by the hills of the
    West,"—
She sang to her boy as he lay on her breast;
"Along its smooth margin thy fathers have played;
Beside its deep waters their ashes are laid."

I wandered afar from the land of my birth,
I saw the old rivers, renowned upon earth,
But fancy still painted that wide-flowing stream
With the many-hued pencil of infancy's dream.

I saw the green banks of the castle-crowned Rhine,
Where the grapes drink the moonlight and change
    it to wine;
I stood by the Avon, whose waves as they glide
Still whisper his glory who sleeps at their side.

But my heart would still yearn for the sound of the
    waves
That sing as they flow by my forefathers' graves;
If manhood yet honors my cheek with a tear,
I care not who sees it, —no blush for it here!

Farewell to the deep-bosomed stream of the West!
I fling this loose blossom to float on its breast;
Nor let the dear love of its children grow cold,
Till the channel is dry where its waters have rolled!

Oliver Wendell Holmes

Riverside

Across the slopes whose wooded spaces hide
The Hudson's sweep, rising more royal than
Above the Tiber that of Hadrian,
A tomb looms domed and dim o'er dusk and tide;
All dreams of alien beauty that abide,
The memory of lands beyond the span
Of seas that sing the deeds of god and man,
May reinspire the soul on Riverside.
And now the mists are falling on the far
Wide silver of the river, and a star
Burns in the pines that crown the Palisades.
Slowly the final streak of sunlight fades,
And Claremont, with the lamps against its white,
Shines like a limpid jewel in the night.

                                        John Myers O'Hara

8. Waterside Life

It Isn't the Town, It's You

If you want to live in the kind of a town
    That's the kind of a town you like,
You needn't slip your clothes in a grip
    And start on a long, long hike.

You'll find elsewhere what you left behind,
    For there's nothing that's really new.
It's a knock at yourself when you knock your town;
    It isn't your town—it's you.

Real towns are not made by men afraid
    Lest somebody else gets ahead.
When everyone works and nobody shirks
    You can raise a town from the dead.

And if while you make your stake
    Your neighbor can make one, too,
Your town will be what you want to see,
    It isn't your town—it's you.

                    R. W. Glover

Voyages I

Above the fresh ruffles of the surf
Bright striped urchins flay each other with sand.
They have contrived a conquest for shell shucks,
And their fingers crumble fragments of baked weed
Gaily digging and scattering.

And in answer to their treble interjections
The sun beats lightning on the waves,
The waves fold thunder on the sand;
And could they hear me I would tell them:

O brilliant kids, frisk with your dog,
Fondle your shells and sticks, bleached
By time and the elements; but there is a line
You must not cross nor ever trust beyond it
Spry cordage of your bodies to caresses
Too lichen-faithful from too wide a breast.
The bottom of the sea is cruel.

Hart Crane

New York

The city is cutting a way,
    The gasmen are hunting a leak;
They're putting down asphalt today,
    To change it for stone in a week.

The builders are raising a wall,
    The wreckers are tearing one down,
Enacting the drama of all
    Our changeable, turbulent town.

For here is an edifice meant
    To stand for an eon or more;
And there is a gospeler's tent,
    And there is a furniture store.

Our suburbs are under the plow,
    Our scaffolds are raw in the sun;
We're drunk and disorderly now,
    But—
'Twill be a great place when it's done!

Arthur Guiterman

A Busy Loneliness

I began to like New York, the racy, adventurous
feel of it at night, and the satisfaction that the
constant flicker of men and women and machines gives
to the restless eye. I liked to walk up Fifth Avenue
and pick out romantic women from the crowd and
imagine that in a few minutes I was going to enter
into their lives, and no one would ever know or
disapprove. Sometimes, in my mind, I followed them
to their apartments on the corners of hidden streets,
and they turned and smiled back at me before they faded
through a door into warm darkness. At the enchanted
metropolitan twilight I felt a haunting loneliness
sometimes, and felt it in others—poor young clerks
who loitered in front of windows waiting until it was
time for a solitary restaurant dinner—young clerks
in the dusk, wasting the most poignant moments of
night and life.

Again at eight o'clock, when the dark lanes of
the Forties were lined five deep with throbbing
taxicabs, for the theater district, I felt a sinking
in my heart. Forms leaned together in the taxis as
they waited, and voices sang, and there was laughter
from unheard jokes, and lighted cigarettes outlined
unintelligible gestures inside. Imagining that I,
too, was hurrying toward gayety and sharing their
intimate excitement, I wished them well.

F. Scott Fitzgerald
The Great Gatsby

A Brief Guide to N. Y.

In New York beautiful girls can become more beautiful
    by going to Elizabeth Arden
And getting stuff put on their faces and waiting
    for it to harden,
And poor girls with nothing to their names
    but a letter or two can get rich and joyous
From a brief trip to their loyous.
So I can say with impunity
That New York is a city of opportunity.
It also has many fine theatres and hotels,
And a lot of taxis, buses, subways and els.
Best of all, if you don't show up at the office
    or a tea nobody will bother their head,
They will just think you are dead.
That's why I really think New York is
    exquisite,
And even nicer to live in than visit.

Ogden Nash

In Schrafft's

Having finished the Blue-Plate Special
And reached the coffee stage,
Stirring her cup she sat,
A somewhat shapeless figure
Of indeterminate age
In an undistinguished hat.

When she lifted her eyes it was plain
That our globular furore,
Our international rout
Of sin and apparatus
And dying men galore,
Was not being bothered about.

Which of the seven heavens
Was responsible her smile
Wouldn't be sure but attested
That, whoever it was, a god
Worth kneeling-to for a while
Had tabernacled and rested.

W. H. Auden

The Sidewalks of New York

Down in front of Casey's old brown wooden stoop
On a summer's evening we formed a merry group;
Boys and girls together, we would sing and waltz
While the "Ginnie" played the organ
On the sidewalks of New York.

That's where Johnny Casey and little Jimmie Crowe,
With Jakey Krause, the baker, who always had the dough,
Pretty Nellie Shannon, with a dude as light as cork,
First picked up the waltz-step
On the sidewalks of New York.

Things have changed since those times,
Some are up in "G,"
Others they are wand'rers, but they all feel just like me.
They'd part with all they've got could they but once more walk
With their best girl and have a twirl
On the sidewalks of New York.

East side, west side, all around the town,
The tots sing "Ring-a-rosie," "London Bridge is falling down,"
Boys and girls together, me and Mamie Rorke
Tripped the light fantastic
On the sidewalks of New York.

Charles B. Lawlor
James W. Blake

Leaving New York

Before I left New York I made arrangements for
securing a passage home in the George Washington packet-
ship, which was advertised to sail in June; that being
the month in which I had determined, if prevented by no
accident in the course of my ramblings, to leave America.

I never thought that going back to England, returning to
all who are dear to me, and to pursuits that have insensibly
grown to be part of my nature, I could have felt so much
sorrow as I endured when I parted at last, on board this ship,
with the friends who had accompanied me from this city.
I never thought the name of any place so far away, and so
lately known, could ever associate itself in my mind with the
crowd of affectionate remembrances that now cluster about it.
There are those in this city who would brighten, to me,
the darkest winter day that ever glimmered and went out in
Lapland; and before whose presence even Home grew dim,
when they and I exchanged that painful word which mingles
with our every thought and deed; which haunts our cradle-heads
in infancy, and closes up the vista of our lives in age.

Charles Dickens
American Notes

A Brief Identification of the Photographs

(The respective page numbers are indicated in bold type)

Manhattan: from the bay **10, 18**; from Liberty Island **15, 80**; from Jersey City **19, 22, 23**; from Brooklyn **24, 39**; from Union City **64, 68**; from West New York **71, 72, 73**; from Weehawken **77**; from the Brooklyn-Queens Expwy. **67**; from Englewood Cliffs **76**; from Queens **79**;

Brooklyn: from the bay **12**; the Heights **13, 17**; the Promenade **189, 204**; from Manhattan **96**; Fulton Street **97, 190, 191**; the Con Edison plant **186**;

The Statue of Liberty Ferry **26**; the Staten Island Ferry **27**; the Statue of Liberty **33, 34, 35**; Ellis Island **36**;

Battery Park: Marine Fire Station **37**; War Memorial **44**; Water gazers **55, 57**; Lovers **211**;

One New York Plaza **38, 246**; the U.S. Treasury Bldg. **40**; Fraunces Tavern and neighbors **42**; the India House **43**; the South Street Seaport **45, 47, 48, 49, 50**; Governors Island **52, 53**; St. Paul's Church **59, 60, 61**; St. Nicholas' Church on Cedar St. and World Trade Center **62**; New York City Hall and Municipal Bldg. **63**;

The Bridges: George Washington Br. **82, 117**; Verrazano Narrows Br. **84, 85, 114**; Brooklyn Br. **89, 91, 92, 95, 100**; Manhattan Br. **93, 94, 98, 99**; Queensboro Br. **101, 102, 103, 104**; Willis Ave. Br. **105**; Williamsburg Br. **106, 107, 108**; Railroad bridge over Randalls Island **109, 122**; Triborough Br. **110, 126**; High Bridge **111**; Throgs Neck Br. **112**; Bronx-Whitestone Br. **113, 127**; Staten Island: Bayonne Br. **119** and Outerbridge Crossing **124, 125**; Henry Hudson Br. **118**; Pulaski Skyway **120, 121**; New Jersey Turnpike **123**; Canal St. Br., West Side Hwy **129**;

The Ships: in the Upper Bay **130, 133, 147**; in the North (Hudson) River **132, 136, 145, 162, 165**; in the Arthur Kill **134, 135**; in the Lower Bay **137, 142**; in Central Park **136, 137, 138, 139, 141, 250**; at the West Side Piers **143, 146, 148, 149, 151, 152, 153, 154, 157, 158, 159, 246, 247**; at Brooklyn Piers **172, 175**;

Tugboats: in the North River **163, 164**; in the Upper Bay **168, 170**; off Hoboken **169, 171**;

Hoboken shipyard **173, 174, 177, 178, 180**; painting an ocean liner **176, 179**; Erie Lackawanna Ry. Station, Hoboken **182, 183**; West Side railroad pier **128**; around the Central R.R. of N.J. Station, Jersey City **25, 182, 185, 187**; Spuyten Duyvil **184, 234**; Columbia Crew **232, 233**;

Manhattan at dusk: from Weehawken **192**; from the Queensboro Br. **196, 197**; from Wards Island **198**; from Brooklyn **199**; from Brooklyn Heights **200**; from the Brooklyn Br. (July 4th) **201**;

Carl Schurz Park **202**; Riverside Park **205, 217**; Ft. Washington Park **207**; Englewood Cliffs **209**; East River Park **210**; Ft. Hamilton Park **212**; Tottenville, Staten Island **213**; Riverside Church and Grant's Tomb **214**; Roosevelt Island Lighthouse **216**; Soldiers' & Sailors' Monument **216**; Sutton Place **218, 227**; Allison Park, Englewood Cliffs **219**; Ft. Tryon Park **220, 221, 222**; The Cloisters **223, 224**; Bronx Community College **225**; Harlem River from High Bridge **226, 228, 229**; Alexander Hamilton Park, Weehawken **230**; Dyckman Street pier **235**; Coney Island **236, 237**; South Beach, Staten Island **239**; Water Street, lower Manhattan **244**; Dead Horse Bay **248**; Mill Basin, Brooklyn **249**; Ships from Ft. Wadsworth **251, 253**.

254

The following has been reprinted by permission of the copyright holders. Most titles to the selections of prose have been added by the editor.

"The Desert Isle" from *Twice Over Lightly, New York Then and Now* © 1972 by Helen Hayes and Anita Loos; "New York, a Vertical but Incomplete City," "The George Washington Bridge: A Place of Radiant Grace," and "A Walk Across the Brooklyn Bridge"—all from *When the Cathedrals Were White* by Le Corbusier © 1947 by Reynal & Hitchcock; "Night Movement—New York" from *Smoke and Steel* © 1948 by Carl Sandburg; "The Supreme American Achievement" and "Around the Great Port" © 1969 by James Morris—all reprinted by permission of Harcourt Brace Jovanovich, Inc.

"A Busy Loneliness" from *The Great Gatsby* by F. Scott Fitzgerald © 1925 by Charles Scribner's Sons; "The Bay" and "The Pin Cushion of Tall Buildings" from *The American Scene* by Henry James © 1945 by Charles Scribner's Sons; "On the Ferryboat" from *Poems 1911–1936* by John Hall Wheelock © 1936 by Charles Scribner's Sons; "The Bridge" from *A Stone, A Leaf, A Door* by Thomas Wolfe © 1945 by Maxwell Perkins (Executor)—all reprinted by permission of Charles Scribner's Sons.

"Vision of the City" and "The Ship" from *A Stone, A Leaf, A Door* by Thomas Wolfe, originally in prose in *The Web and the Rock* by Thomas Wolfe © 1939 by Maxwell Perkins (Executor); "The Quest of the Fair Medusa" from *You Can't Go Home Again* by Thomas Wolfe © 1934, 1937, 1938, 1939, 1940 by Maxwell Perkins (Executor); "Manhattan is Like a Poem" from *Here Is New York* © 1949 by E.B. White—all reprinted by permission of Harper & Row, Publishers, Inc.

"The Harbor Dawn," "To Brooklyn Bridge," and "Voyages I" from *Collected Poems and Selected Letters and Prose of Hart Crane* © 1933, 1958, 1966 by Liveright Publishing Corp., reprinted by permission of the publisher.

"The Hooker" from *Back Where I Came From* by A.J. Liebling © 1938 by Jean Stafford Liebling (Executrix).

"Earth, Water, Sky, Men" from *City Development—Studies in Disintegration and Renewal* © 1945 by Lewis Mumford.

"From the Ferryboat" and "Dusk" from *Manhattan Transfer* by John Dos Passos © 1953 by Elizabeth H. Dos Passos (Executrix).

"New York" from *Ballads of Old New York* by Arthur Guiterman © 1939 by Vida Lindo Guiterman (Executrix).

"In Schrafft's" from *Collected Shorter Poems 1927–1957* by W.H. Auden © 1966 by Random House, Inc., reprinted by permission of the publisher.

"A Brief Guide to New York" from *Verses from 1929 On* by Ogden Nash © 1959 by Little, Brown & Co., reprinted by permission of the publisher.

"Luck" by Wilfrid Gibson from *The Sea, Ships and Sailors* collected by William Cole, reprinted by permission of Mr. Michael Gibson and Macmillan, London and Basingstoke.

Acknowledgment is made for the following material included in this book:

"Old St. Paul's" by Arthur Upson (permission originally from Keith Clark), "Riverside" by John Myers O'Hara (permission originally from Messrs. Smith and Sale), and "New Colossus" by Emma Lazarus—all from *The Book of New York Verse* collected by Hamilton Fish Armstrong © 1917 by Hamilton Fish Armstrong.

"It Isn't the Town, It's You" by R. W. Glover, "The Bridge Builder" by Will Allen Dromgoole, and "The Sidewalks of New York" by Charles B. Lawlor and James W. Blake—all from *The Best Loved Poems of the American People* selected by Hazel Felleman © 1936 by Doubleday & Co. Inc.

"On the Quay" by John Joy Bell from *The Home Book of Verse* edited by Burton E. Stevenson © 1926 by Henry Holt & Co.

"Sailing Day Scenes" from *The New York City Sketches of Stephen Crane* edited by R. W. Stallman and E. R. Hageman © 1966 by New York University Press.

"Specimen Days" and "Democratic Vistas" from *The Collected Writings of Walt Whitman* edited by Floyd Stovall © 1963 by New York University Press.

"Mannahatta," "Crossing Brooklyn Ferry," "City of Ships," "After the Sea Ship," and "Song for All Seas, All Ships" from *Leaves of Grass* by Walt Whitman © 1900 by David McKay.

"City Streets" from *Songs of Manhattan* by Morris Abel Beer © 1918 by Cornhill & Co.

"Manhattan's Dear Isle" by W. F. Spicer from *Naval Songs* collected by Rear Admiral Stephen B. Luce © 1902 by the U.S. Navy.

"At Sea" and "A Sea Song from the Shore" from *The Poems and Prose Sketches of James Whitcomb Riley* © 1898 by James Whitcomb Riley.

"The Hudson" from *The Poetical Works of Oliver Wendell Holmes* © 1908 by Houghton Mifflin & Co.

"Wall Street, South Street" and "Leaving New York" from *American Notes* by Charles Dickens © 1891 by Dodd Mead & Co.

"The City of the Future" from *The Future in America* by H.G. Wells © 1934 by Herbert George Wells.

"A Scene on the Banks of the Hudson" and "Hymn of the City" from *The Poetical Works of William Cullen Bryant* © 1883 by D. Appleton & Co.

Acknowledgments

Sidney Rapoport, Peter Stanford, Yustin Wallrap and colleagues,

Harry Amdur, Stevan Baron, Kent Barwick, Shirly Bressler,
Richard H. Buford, Joseph Cantalupo, Norman H. Cohen,
George Costa, Eugene Feldman, Eugena Flatow,
Larry Friedman, Christopher Harris, Norman Krupit,
Starling R. Lawrence, Loren Lieberman, Justine Mee,
Klaus Moser, David Morton, Gretel J. Neuberger,
Michael A. Oser, Richard W. Pelak, David Reichberg,
Alan Stark, Marshall Streibert, Roberta Vrona,
Christopher Weiman, Henry Weiman, James M. West,

Elaine Donnelly, Helen Earle, Hoyt Evans, Thomas O'Brien,

Alan Frese, Daian Frese, Jean Frey, Earl Gardner,
Mary Makras, James O'Connor, Lee Tobin.

McAllister Brothers, Inc., Moran Towing & Transportation Co., Inc.,
Allan and Gray Corporation, Bethlehem Steel Corporation,
Chandris America Lines, Inc., Costa Line, Cunard Line Ltd.,
Farrell Lines Inc., Home Lines, Inc., Holland America Cruises Inc.,
A. Horowitz & Son, Prudential Lines, Inc.

Committee on the City Waterfront and Waterways
Municipal Arts Society
New York City Planning Commission
Port Authority of New York and New Jersey
South Street Seaport Museum